A Fire in My Hands

Poems by **Gary Soto**

A Fire in My Hands

Revised
and
Expanded
Edition

Harcourt, Inc.

Orlando   Austin   New York   San Diego   Toronto   London

For information about permission to reproduce selections from this book,
write to Permissions, Houghton Mifflin Harcourt Publishing Company,
215 Park Avenue South, New York, New York 10003.

www.hmhbooks.com

"Oranges," "Black Hair," "That Girl," "Hitchhiking with a Friend,"
"In August," "Envying the Children of San Francisco," "Teaching Numbers,"
"Brown Girl, Blonde Okie," and "Kearney Park," from *Gary Soto:
New and Selected Poems* by Gary Soto, 1995, Chronicle Books.
Reprinted by permission of the author and publisher.

"Inheritance" from *A Natural Man* by Gary Soto, 1999, Chronicle Books.
Reprinted by permission of the author and publisher.

"Some Words about Time" from *Ploughshares,* Spring 2005, vol. 31, no. 1, edited
by Martín Espada. Reprinted by permission of the author and publisher.

The author wishes to thank Adam Lowry at Chronicle Books
and Lindy Humphreys, formerly at Chronicle Books.

Library of Congress Cataloging-in-Publication Data
Soto, Gary.
A fire in my hands/Gary Soto.—Rev. and expanded ed.
p. cm.
1. Central Valley (Calif.: Valley)—Poetry. 2. Central Valley (Calif.: Valley)—
Anecdotes. 3. Poets, American—20th century—Anecdotes. 4. Mexican
American poets—Anecdotes. 5. Mexican American youth—Poetry.
6. Mexican Americans—Anecdotes. 7. Soto, Gary—Anecdotes. I. Title.
PS3569.O72F5 2006
811'.54—dc22   2005024610
ISBN 978-0-15-205564-6

Text set in Meridien
Designed by April Ward

DOC 10 9 8 7
4500449522

Printed in the United States of America

To Jim Blasingame
and Carol Lem,
master teachers

Contents

Introduction

I began writing poetry while I was in college in the early 1970s. One day I was in the library, working on a term paper for geography (my major at the time), when by chance, I came across an anthology of contemporary poetry called *The New American Poetry, 1945–1960*. I leafed through it, bewildered that none of the poems rhymed. And a good many had subjects that didn't appear to be "poetic." Wasn't poetry about waves crashing on the shore and stopping a sleigh on a winter night to admire the snowy drifts against a moonlit rock wall? One poem particularly struck me; it was Gregory Corso's "Marriage," which is one young man's account of getting ready to meet his future in-laws. The tone is casual, and in fact, nearly irreverent toward the age-old custom of a young man asking for the daughter's hand in marriage. In the poem the young man is forced to wear a tie and make nice chitchat with his future in-laws—at heart he's really a rebel and would rather be dressed in jeans and a leather jacket, with slicked-back hair and smelling faintly of motor oil. The poem is wild, even rude, and nothing like the rhyme-and-meter poetry I had read in high school. I had always assumed that poetry was flowery writing, but this anthology contained direct and sometimes shocking poetry about dogs, junked cars, rundown houses, and loud TVs. I checked the book out, curious to read more.*

Soon afterward, I started filling a notebook with my own poems. At first I was scared, partly because no one in my family had ever tried to write a poem, and I was worried about what they would think of my new activity. Also, I realized the seriousness of an attempt to write, especially after I enrolled in my first poetry workshop and my teacher began to bellow his complaints about my sloppiness. (Oh, how right he was.) I soon gave up geography to study poetry, which a good many friends said offered no future. I ignored them to reconstruct the past, which has always been a source of poetry for me.

When I first studied poetry, I was single-minded. I woke to poetry and went to bed with poetry. I memorized poems, read English poets because I was told they would help shape my poems, and read classical Chinese poetry because I was told that it would add clarity to my work. But I was most taken by Spanish and Latin American poets, particularly Pablo Neruda. My favorites of his were the odes—long, short-lined poems celebrating common things

* This anthology of poetry was subsequently given to me as a gift at a formal occasion, presented by a librarian at Fresno City College. She had read somewhere that the collection had changed the direction of my life. How true.

like tomatoes, socks, scissors, birds, and artichokes. I felt joyful when I read these odes, and confident because the poems seemed splendid examples for my own work. When I began to write my own poems, I tried to remain faithful to the common things of my childhood—dogs, alleys, school-yard fights, my baseball mitt, curbs where I played with red ants, and the fruits of the Valley, especially the orange. I wanted to give these things life and to write so well that my poems would express their simple beauty.

I also admired our own country's poetry. I saw that our American poets often wrote about places where they grew up or places that impressed them deeply. James Wright wrote about Ohio and West Virginia, William Stafford about the Northwest, Gary Snyder about the Sierra Nevada, and Robert Frost, perhaps our greatest treasure, about New Hampshire and the surrounding states. I decided to write about the San Joaquin Valley, where my hometown, Fresno, is located. Some of my poems are stark observations of human violence—burglaries, muggings, fistfights—while others are spare images of nature—the orange groves and vineyards, the Kings River, the sloughs and bogs, the Sequoias with their old-growth redwoods. I fell in love with the Valley, both its ugliness and its beauty, and quietly wrote poems about it to share with others.

I like to think of my poems as a "working life," by which I mean that my poems are about commonplace, everyday things—baseball games, an evening walk, a boyhood friendship, first love, marriage, fatherhood, a tree, rock 'n' roll, the homeless, dancing. The poems keep alive the small moments that add up to a large moment: life itself.

More than a quarter century has passed since I left college. I had no idea that I would write so much or that more than a few friends would read what I wrote. Some of you will read these poems and will want to write your own. Good. Poems should feed into other poems—a needle passing a stitch through cloth. My advice to young poets is "Look to your own lives." What are your life stories? Can you remember incidents from your childhood? Some of you may argue that your life is boring, that nothing has happened, that everything interesting happens far away. Not so. Your lives are at work, too.

Each of the poems in this collection is preceded by an anecdote. In the back of the book, I answer questions about poetry. Your answers one day might differ from mine, and we will attribute this to your own growth. Each poet works differently. But the task is the same—to get the language right so that the subject of the poem will live.

A Fire in My Hands

As a kid, I was no good at baseball. Many of my summers were spent watching games from the bleachers and rooting for a player who was Mexican American, like me.

Black Hair

At eight I was brilliant with my body.
In July, that ring of heat
We all jumped through, I sat in the bleachers
Of Romain Playground, in the lengthening
Shade that rose from our dirty feet.
The game before us was more than baseball.
It was the figure of Hector Moreno,
Quick and hard with turned muscles,
His crouch the one I assumed before an altar
Of worn baseball cards, in my bedroom.

I came here because I was Mexican,
A stick of brown light in love with those
Who could do it—the triple and hard slide,
The glove, eating balls in double plays.
What could I do with my 60 pounds, my shyness,
My black torch of hair about to go out?
Father was dead, his face no longer
Present at the kitchen table or smiling down on our sleep,
And Mother was the terror of mouths
Twisting hurt in sickly nightmares.

1

In the bleachers I was brilliant with my body,
Waving players in and stomping my feet,
Growing sweaty in the presence of white shirts.
I chewed sunflower seeds. I drank water
And bit my arm nervously through the late innings.
When Hector lined balls into deep
Center, in my mind I rounded the bases
With him, my face flared, my hair lifting
Beautifully, because we were coming home
Into the arms of brown people.

It All Makes Sense

A shovel in rain, a baseball in the flower bed,
A tree that shrugged off its leaves,
And the fake beard you pressed to your face one Halloween
When you strode stiffly as Frankenstein—boo.

Things you find in the yard. They make sense,
The shovel for instance. One day
You tried to dig up the tree in the middle of the lawn,
Right where you wanted to make room to wind up

And practice pitching fastballs into the stomach
Of an old mattress, the same old mattress
Where you first tried on your fake beard,
Sneezed and said, "It tickles."

You think about this as you grip the rain-swollen baseball.
You eye the mattress, still leaning against the fence.
Your anger could melt snow. You recall when

You were five, jumping up and down on that mattress,
Cheap fun until you hit your head on the ceiling
And saw stars, then blood around the stars—
No, those were your front teeth in your palms.

You now shiver in autumn, narrow an eye at the mattress,
And let the baseball fly at it,
The cause of your early childhood grief.
But the baseball sails over the mattress, the fence,

And breaks glass in the neighbor's yard.
Through the fence slats,
You see the bear of a man still in his pajamas yelling
As the door slides open around glass.
Was he hibernating? Sleeping in a recliner big as an elephant?
Well, he's awake now.

But smart you, you put on the fake beard,
And tiptoe away with your head hunched into your shoulders,
Stepping into puddles and leaving no tracks
That a bear could follow.

That Girl

The public library was saying things
In so many books
And I, a Catholic boy
In a green sweater,
Was reading the same page
A hundred times.
A girl was in my way,
And she was at the other end
Of the oak table,
Her hands like doves
On the encyclopedia, E–G.
Was she looking up England,
I thought, or Germany
Before the start of the war?
She'll copy from that book,
Cursive like waves
Riding to the shore,
And tomorrow walk across lawns
In a public school dress
With no guilt pulling at an ear.
And me? I'll kick
My Catholic shoes through
Leaves, stand in the

When I first started liking girls, about the time I was in seventh grade, I often couldn't concentrate on my homework, which I did at the public library. I would look up, and there would be a girl I could like.

Cloakroom and eat
A friend's lunch. My work
Was never finished.
My maps were half-colored,
History a stab in the dark,
And fractions the inside
Of a pocket watch
Spilled on my desk.
I was no good. And who do
I blame? That girl, of course.
When she scribbled a pink
Eraser and her ponytails
Bounced like skirts,
I looked up, gazed for what
My mother and sister could not
Offer, then returned to
The same sentence: *The Nile*
Is the longest river in the world.
A pencil rolled from the
Table when she clicked open
Her binder. I looked up,
Gazed, looked back down:
The Nile is the longest river . . .

Lost in a Small Town

Where's my watch?
Ticking like a bomb under the bed.

Where's my mouse?
Out of its cage
And pressed in a trap.

Where's Joe Montana's jersey?
On the back of an Alaskan husky named Rex,
And looking better on his body than yours.

It's a rainy Saturday,
And you're at a loss for something to do.
You stop at the baseball diamond
Where a bully with green teeth made you eat grass.
Two girls looked on, and you actually cried.
(You don't know this, but the bully's green teeth
Are gone now—someone bigger than him smacked him
With a board.)

There were days in my youth
when I was bored and would walk
around Fresno, in search of something
meaningful. There were times when
a stray dog would tag along.

You walk the length of your town—twice.
You can do without a watch, the pet rodent,
The NFL jersey. But where is love? Perhaps in the alley,
Blowing like a newspaper with good and bad news,
Or perhaps love is the girl in curlers peeking
From behind a curtain.

You walk with your hands like gavels in your jacket.
A stray dog follows. Maybe this is love,
You think, a dog with one blue eye and one brown eye.
You're mismatched friends but what
The heck. He stops to lick
Rain from the tops of your shoes.
Suddenly you know in your heart
That somewhere, sometime in his short dog life,
A bully dog bigger than him made him cower
To the ground as two Lassie dogs watched
Before trotting away.

You shrug your shoulders, shiver.
What are you doing but looking at yourself,
With rain ticking on your shoulders.

Oranges

The first time I went out
With a girl, I was thirteen,
Cold, and weighted down
With two oranges in my jacket.
December. Frost cracked
Beneath my steps, my breath
Before me, then gone,
As I walked toward
This girl's house, the one whose
Porch light burned yellow
Night and day, in any weather.
A dog barked at me, until
She came out pulling
On her gloves, face bright
With makeup. I smiled,
Touched her shoulder, and led
Her down the street, across
A used car lot and a line
Of newly planted trees,
Until we were standing
In front of a drugstore.

We entered, the tiny bell
Bringing a saleslady
Down a narrow aisle of goods.
I turned to the candies
Tiered like bleachers,
And asked my girl what she wanted—
Light in her eyes, a smile
Starting at the corners
Of her mouth. I fingered
A nickel in my pocket,
And when she lifted a chocolate
That cost a dime,
I didn't say anything.
I took the nickel from
My pocket, then an orange,
And set them quietly on
The counter. When I looked up
The saleslady's eyes met mine,
And held them, knowing
Very well what it was about,
Love, I mean.

Outside the drugstore,
A few cars racing past,
Fog hanging like old
Coats between the wintry trees.

I took my girl's hand
In mine for two short blocks,
Then released it to let
Her unwrap her chocolate.
I peeled my orange
That was so bright against
The gray of December
That, from some distance,
Someone might have thought
I was making a fire in my hands.

Often it's hit-or-miss when we try to connect romantically with another person. You may like another person's face or figure, but once that person starts talking you may be startled by what comes out.

Mating Season

She said, Autumn is when you hold hands.
He said, It's the start of football season.

She said, Is that burning leaves I smell?
He said, I think it's a hot dog.

She said, I like movies that make me sad.
He said, I get sad when Coach sits me on the bench.

She said, Christmas is my favorite season.
He said, Me too—that's when I get money from my grandma.

(The girl looked skyward, winced.
The boy scraped something yellow from the corner
Of his mouth—mustard.)

She said, My dog died rescuing a baby from a burning house.
He said, I had a dog who could juggle tennis balls—really!

She said, I would like to know French.
He said, Isn't France where they like really old cheese?

———

She said, I'm a Capricorn.

He said, Is that like being a vegan?

They smiled, certain of each other,

And started walking down the street,

Hands almost touching,

Each saying in her heart, his heart:

You'll do.

Learning to Bargain

Summer. Flies knitting

Filth on the window,

A mother calling a son home . . .

At the window, I gaze

Toward the street: dusk,

A neighbor kid sharpening

A stick at the curb.

I go outside and sit

Next to him without saying

A word. When he looks

Up, his eyes dark as flies . . .

I ask about the cat, the one dead

Among the weeds in the alley.

"Yeah, I did it," he admits,

And stares down at his feet,

Then my feet. "What do you want?"

"A dime," I say. Without

Looking at me, he gets

Up, goes behind his house,

And returns with two Coke bottles.

"These make a dime." He sits
At the curb, his shoulders
So bony they could be wings
To lift him so far. "Don't tell."
He snaps a candy into halves
And we eat in silence.

One summer day I looked up and saw a blimp hovering above the pickle factory near our house. My friends and I were not allowed there, but because it was Saturday, we thought we had the run of the yard.

In August

A blimp was above me
And then gone,
Like all I would ever know.
Like Father with hands in my hair,
Like Uncle on the porch
With his sickly arms and little else.
I walked into the alley looking up
Until it wasn't the sky before
Me, but a plum tree,
Its dark fruit notched and open
Where birds ate. I climbed
Onto a branch, scavenged,
And dropped with two in each hand.
I walked from the alley
To Coleman Pickle
Where brother, friends, tiny sister
Were standing in barrels,
Pickles in their hands
And saying, "They're good,
Better than plums." I climbed

Into a barrel and fished for one

With my toes. But I stopped

When I saw a blimp

Pass quietly as a cloud,

Its shadow dark enough to sleep

Or dream in. We watched

With food in our mouths,

All wondering, until it was above us

And then gone,

Like all we would ever know.

All the Luck

I was in love with the homecoming queen
And she with some muscle in a letterman's jacket,
Medals dangling like fishing lures on his mountainous chest.

And me? I wore a hairnet and served chili beans
On plastic dishes, and with Arturo
Rinsed those dishes in the heaven of steam.
I got extra credit for my effort, plus all I could eat.
And in biology, my chin in my hand,
I watched the sky with its cargo of clouds
Once more bypassing our desert town. I tried
To be a good student. I lowered my good eye
   into microscopes
And confirmed that we were made of cells—
The teacher, a guy in a soggy bow tie,
Told us we were made of cells.
Sure enough, when I lay a piece of fingernail
Under the lens I could see it was true.

Because of junk food, I multiplied like a cell,
And hung with Arturo by the dry school fountain
Where we flipped pennies for fun. No one cared for us.

———————

One Wednesday in biology, a cloud stopped
Over our school and kindly filled our fountain—
Just as I was yanking a strand of hair
From my head to see if that part of me was cell stuff, too.

When class ended, I hurried to see our fountain.
I sighed. I believe I leaked a tear,
Me, the boy with a crushed leaf for a heart,
All because I discovered not a beautiful scene of autumn
But trash floating on the surface.
I flipped a penny into the dark waters for good luck
And got my wish—the homecoming queen
Was sailing slowly past on a parade float,
Practice for the real thing that evening.
She was waving "Hello, Hello."
But as the parade float pulled away,
For me, one of the nobodies,
It was unmistakably "Good-bye, Good-bye."

How You Gave Up Root Beer

The shame of pounding back a root beer at eight o'clock
In the morning, then the sudden hiccup
That pulls the brew into your nostrils,
Twin faucets releasing foam and liquid
Down your upper lip.

All of this is happening
While the girl you like more than your own life
Turns the hallway corner,
Bouncy girl from history class.
She sees you, her hand coming up to cover her mouth.
She squeaks, "That's ugly."

You close your eyes,
But that doesn't stop the liquid from plunging
Over the ridge of your lip and down your chin.
It would wet your Adam's apple
Except smart you have squeegeed
That sweet runoff
With a finger.

––––––––––

The girl clip-clops away,
Leaving you holding a soda can in your hand.
You could kick yourself and instead kick down the hall,
You the donkey boy.

You can't blame anyone else.
Your mother warned you
Repeatedly about drinking soda in the morning,
And scolded you about how it destroys teeth
And adds handfuls of wobbly fat to a waist.

Bad son, you failed to listen.

I play favors with my food as I'm a glutton for enchiladas suizas and other Mexican dishes. Here are a few playful rules regarding the etiquette of eating.

Eating Mexican Food

Rule #1

Don't pick up the tortilla
With your fork.

Rule #2

Salsa—red ants
Marching on your tongue.

It's okay to scream into your napkin.

Rule #3

Keep things clean—
Wipe the plate's face with a napkin of tortilla.

Rule #4

With *posole* soup,

The corn arrives smiling.

By the end of the meal,

It's toothless as an old man.

As for you, roll your tongue across your own teeth

Like a wiper blade pushing down dead

Yellow insects.

Rule #5

It's okay to prop your elbows on the table.

And if an ant comes to see,

Show kindness—

A single grain of rice will do.

Rule #6

The menu's in Spanish?

Nothing wrong with pointing.

Rule #7

You're friendlier than you think.

A fly, mostly eyes, circles your plate.

When the fly sets down,

He scrubs his hands for dinner.

Offer this uninvited guest a chip.

A little kick-butt salsa will open his eyes even wider.

Saturday
at the Canal

I'm seventeen, at the canal, and looking west where San Francisco and Oakland lie on the fringes of my imagination. I want to get out of town and see for myself what the world is like.

I was hoping to be happy by seventeen.
School was a sharp check mark in the roll book,
An obnoxious tuba playing at noon because our team
Was going to lose again that night. The teachers were
Too close to dying to understand. The hallways
Stank of poor grades and unwashed hair. Thus,
A friend and I sat watching the water on Saturday,
Neither of us talking much, just warming ourselves
By hurling large rocks at a tumbleweed
And feeling awful because San Francisco was nothing
But a postcard on our bedroom walls. We wanted to go there,
Hitchhike under the last migrating birds
And be with people who knew more than three chords
On a guitar. We didn't drink or smoke,
But our hair was shoulder length, wild when
The wind picked up and the shadows of
This loneliness gripped loose dirt. By bus or car,
By the sway of the train over a long bridge,
We wanted to get out. The years froze
As we sat on the bank. Our eyes followed the water,
White-tipped but dark underneath, racing out of town.

October

A cold day, though it's only October,
And the grass has grayed
Like the frost that hardened it
This morning.

And this morning
After the wind left
With its pile of clouds,
The broken fence steamed, sunlight spread
Like seed from one field
To another, out of a bare sycamore
Sparrows lifted above the ridge.

In the ditch an owl shuffled into a nest
Of old leaves and cotton,
A black tassel of lizard flapping
From its beak. Mice
And ants gathered under the flat ground
And slipped downward like water.
A coyote squatted behind granite,
His ears tilting toward the rustle
Of winter's icy teeth.

Kearney Park

True Mexicans or not, let's open our shirts
And dance, a spark of heels
Chipping at the dusty cement. The people
Are shiny as the sea. They turn
To the clockwork of rancheras,
The accordion wheezing, the drum-tap
Of work rising and falling.
Let's dance with our hats in hand.
The sun is behind the trees,
Behind my stutter of awkward steps
With a woman who is a brilliant arc of smiles,
An armful of falling water. Her skirt
Flares. My arms flop, and we spin, dip,
And laugh into each other's faces—
Faces that could be famous
On the coffee table of my *abuelita*.
But, I see, Grandma is here, at the park,
With a soda at her feet, clapping and shouting,
"Baile, hijo, baile!" Laughing, I bend, slide,
And throw up a great cloud of dust,
Until, like magic, the girl and I are no more.

One Sunday my girlfriend and I came across dancers while we were walking through the park. We joined them, shyly at first, because we didn't know how to dance very well. But in no time we were kicking up our heels to the music.

I never received an allowance. If I wanted money for a movie or a soda, I had to earn it. Often I went door-to-door selling oranges. In this poem, I'm looking for sympathy.

How to Sell Things

First, you need a dog
Chased hungry by a cloud
All night, fur over
His eyes, breath white
In the early morning
That has sent you door
To door with a sack
Of oranges. Two for
A nickel, you might say,
Two for a dime if it's
A rich lady who's known
Steak and roses in her time.
Play it up. Backhand
Your nose, shiver like a leaf,
And look down at your ugly shoes.
A hard sell? Then
Call the dog to roll over,
Whine, and raise a paw in salute.
If the rich lady is still
With hands on hips

And shaking her head,
Then call for the dog
To speak a few words
On his back—tiny legs
Prancing in the air.
Make sure it's Sunday,
When God is looking around
For something to do.

Hope

Maybe the dog I loved best will limp

Up the street and fall at my feet,

Not really hurt, just tired. "Smoky,"

I cry, and in crying send the sparrows

In the tree a limb higher. "I missed you,

I really missed you. Where did you go?"

I peel back his eyelids and view

An adventure—oh, how he dodged cars

And dipped his tired paws in puddles, how

He slept in ditches and bit a tribe of fleas

Camping in his fur. I see him topple

A garbage can and a rat with long whiskers

Run between his feet. I see him living

With a kind old woman by a railroad.

She ate a lot of stew, and shared her stew,

Until her mean son drove her away,

Leaving Smoky to wag his tail in dust.

"Oh, Smoky," I sob. I scan

The full story in his eyes. I see my dog

Sniffing the air, his nostrils flaring

For the scent of home, my home
With newspapers piled up on the roof
And duct tape on the broken front window.
Now my dog's collapsed at my feet.
"You're home," I say to Smoky,
"And you're never going to leave again."
True, our house appears abandoned
Ever since Dad left and left an oil stain on the drive.
But I'm here in this house of ours,
My mother and little brother are here,
And aren't those daffodils below the window
A sign of spring? I hug my dog,
Who disappeared when I was nine.
Now I'm twelve, a dodger of cars,
An ambler of ditch banks. When I bend
Over and bring him into my arms,
What do I feel but the weight of fur
And three lost years.

The Function of Two E-mail Accounts

Once, I sent an e-mail to myself
And ate a sandwich while watching two kids
On trikes run over a watermelon rind on the sidewalk.
Boy, looks like fun, I told myself, licked the tips
Of my fingers, and then hurried to my bedroom—
My older brother's poster of The Hulk was snarling at me.

Casually, I typed in my account ThE bOy,
A tricky way of hoarding my identity,
And tapped in my password *********.
I cracked my knuckles. There it is,
I told myself, the message from me to me,
And—wait!—three mysterious other messages.
I opened them up, one by one,
And discovered I'm not too young to own a credit card,
That starting at $150.00 (plus airfare)
Hawaii, our glorious fiftieth state, was waiting for me,
And that with the signature from one, semilucid parent
You can become a foreign exchange student.

I pushed away from my computer.

Big ideas exploded in the alleys of my brain.

Oh, how I could use a credit card to buy jackets

For the whole school,

And what's wrong with a coconut falling on your head,

Provided girls swish in their grassy skirts a moment later.

And me as a foreign exchange student?

I pictured myself rolling spaghetti on a large spoon

While sitting at a long wooden table.

I next opened the message

From me to me . . . *nada*. My message was gone,

A blank space on the screen. I looked toward the ceiling

And imagined my message circling blindly in space,

Where it was colliding with other lost messages.

In case it pops up on your screen, don't dismiss it as junk!

It's a call from my heart that says: I'm twelve, four feet nine,

And weigh eighty-six pounds. My favorite color

Is blue. Onions in hamburgers

Make me burp. I sometimes respond to Dufus.

Write me and I'll be your friend.

Christopher Smart, the eighteenth-century poet, loved his cat Jeoffry, who had many talents, among them the talent to juggle a cork. I pay homage to Smart and all cats of the world.

Mr. Meow

For I will consider Mr. Meow,

For he is a cat with a blade of grass under his paw,

For the grass is gone in three licks,

For he blinks, for he purrs the stomach of plenty,

For he yawns when the clock strikes noon.

It's noon now. Mr. Meow rises,

His front legs stretched forward in homage to his shadow.

And for the sake of his pink tongue

He prances to his water bowl.

He pokes his nose at the image of himself

And his whiskers rake the surface.

Done, Mr. Meow braves the jungly yard,

For he is a cat with seven days off,

For he is the warden of the sparrow and the pear-shaped
robin,

For he is the prince of the flea in his left shoulder,

For he is the conductor of that bell under his chin,

For briefly he is the sentry at an anthill gone cold.

Mr. Meow seizes the day.

He steps through hillside grass that whispers at his thighs.

He shakes the flea from his left shoulder to his right knee.

He nudges the bell and the birds sail into the trees.

He drinks from his paw print filled with rain.

He sits with his tail like a question mark behind him,

For he must consider his duties:

For one catch a leaf in midair,

For two avoid all roads with yellow stripes,

For three roll to his back and pedal his legs,

For four spark the stockings of a nicely dressed woman,

For five perk up ears when a Chihuahua barks,

For six venture to the fence and meow to the bark,

For seven climb a tree and meow to get down,

For eight blink sleepily at the embers in the fireplace,

For nine snag his collar on a branch,

For ten hurry from rain and meow at the back door.

Mr. Meow knows best. He loves all of his nine lives.

He knows the kindness of a stranger's caress,

For his father's father sailed on the Nile,

For his mother's mother hauled her young in her teeth,

For snow taught him cold, fire taught him Stay Back,

For he stepped into fog and once disappeared,

For he learned dizziness from a grandfather clock's pendulum.

True, Mr. Meow was trained to sniff for mice.

True, he befriends the toad and the toad's cousin, the tadpole.

True, he will consider what falls beneath the kitchen table.

His fears are rain, and bats with reddish eyes.

His happiness is tossing the bottle cap and catching it
in his fangs.

But what more does he know, what more to consider?

For in idleness he fools with a walnut,

For his head shovels into a nice girl's lap,

For he cries but not too loudly,

For he can raise a leg over his head,

For he sports his gray coat,

For his tail whips him to action when a wheel comes too close,

For he reigns tall on the throne of a garbage can,

For his eyes shine in the closet,

For he climbs a curtain for a better view of the sofa,

For if a dam breaks he can swim with his ears pulled back,

For he creeps to a dirty sock under the bed,

For under the bed he dusts with his belly,

For his engines run,

For he comes running when the refrigerator door is opened.

Spying a plate of chicken wings,

He'll reach in with washed and eager paws

And, unlike the dog, devour politely just what he can eat!

My grandfather was from Mexico
and came to the United States during
the 1920s, when he settled in Fresno.
There he met my grandmother.
Together they raised six children.
Here I offer him praise.

Inheritance

Retired, my grandfather chewed frijoles like a camel,
His large jaw churning,
His tortilla a napkin at the edge of his plate.
He ate alone, or nearly alone,
A parakeet the size of a swollen thumb
Glancing in a mirror. When the parakeet rang its bell,
Grandfather moved his camel head and scolded, "Shaddup."
The bird was not his,
But Grandmother's, hall-shuffler in pink slippers,
Beater of rugs and dusty work clothes,
Beautician dying her hair black on shadow-cold mornings.

Nights, Grandfather sat in his recliner
With the thorn-sharp doily pressed against his neck.
He sat while the TV shuffled light in his face
And the radio plugged his ears with mariachis.
In the kitchen, the washer shivered a load of whites,
Plates rattled, black tea rolled its knuckles in a saucepan.
When the telephone rang its loud threats,
He turned his camel head and shouted, "Shaddup!"

He wanted the peace of a green lawn, lost at dusk,
And a summer burst of squash on whiskery vines.
He believed in water, water of morning
And of night, water of sprinklers set at the curb.
He knew how summer heat suckled trees and lawns.
This worried him. How it could dry up,
Life included, dry up in the time you turned your back
And flicked a grain from under a fingernail.

Grandfather rose late,
The day already sobbing heat in the garden.
He sliced a lemon and in the bathroom
Rubbed its sweet acids under his arms,
The scent that would follow him through the day.
The squeezed lemon collapsed into a frown,
And he was ready. Ready for what? He ate
And drank coffee, his mouth pleated on each deep sip.
He studied roses, the wicked queens of his garden,
And raked puckered oranges into a herd
Of croquet balls. "Keep things green, *mi'jo*,"
He repeated to me about life.
Water surged in the flower bed
And into the volcanic peaks
Of anthills, the silt as fine as gold.
Grandfather was a simple man, a work-worn camel

With a busy jaw. Our inheritance was a late afternoon
With my small hand under his, the garden hose splashing
For the good of the living.

One day a friend and I decided to hitchhike to the ocean. We were young men in search of adventure. When we were left off on the side of a road, the windswept field seemed strangely familiar, yet new, and the gray sky was haunting. We walked over the crunch of gravel, feeling utterly free at being far from home.

Hitchhiking with a Friend

On Highway 41, out of Stratford,

The sky lengthens magically

When you're 19, the first time

On the road. And if you're

With a friend, the birds lift

And never come down in the same place.

I found myself out there with Samuel,

Both of us hungry as fire

As we kicked rocks under a wide sky.

We both believed in the notion of beauty.

It was that word, and others,

That had us pointing

To windmills, burnt slopes, and sullen cows,

The trees irresponsible with their shadows.

And it was the eagerness of grass

Under wind, a tumbleweed

Moving, a paper bag moving,

And our minds clear as water

Pooled on roadsides. We went

On for hours. The gravel
Turned under our march,
Until the landscape meant less,
And we grew tired. A banged-up
Truck stopped for us
And the driver's giddy dog licked
And nuzzled our necks
All through the foothills toward Pismo.
Two hours, two sodas we raised like trumpets,
And the sky became hazed with mist.
When we saw a rough cut
Of sea through cypress trees,
We tilted our heads, nudged
Each other's ribs at the blue
Waves that would end at our feet.

All of us have our limits, and sometimes we learn them early in life. Sometimes it takes years to grasp our limitations because we're stubborn. What could I do well in my early life? Pet a dog's nose, and not much more. And there are days now when I can't do anything right, not even fry an egg.

Knowing Your Limits

I recall the brick wall

I could have gone around.

Instead, I curled my little fingers

And hooked my toes into the cracks.

I failed to climb over and went away

To pet a dog's nose that poked through

The slats of a wooden fence.

The dog pressed his body against

The fence, and from the reflection

Of his eyeball I saw the brick wall behind me.

I scratched the dog's chin.

I left the yard.

The whistle at Sun-Maid Raisin blew,

Scattering birds from a wire fence.

I dared myself to walk

In front of Mr. Drake's house,

Old Man Drake who walked

As if on stilts to his outhouse.

Next, I jumped into a dead leaf fire in the gutter,

But the leaves down below were still smoldering.
I hurried home on the blades of blistered feet
And petted the nose of a dog, something
I knew I could do right.

Today I recall the wall, the hot ash.
I go into the kitchen to strike an egg against the edge
Of a black pan.
Don't break, I say to the egg,
Whose white edges flap like a rug.
When the yolk breaks and slowly
Bleeds, I want to kill this egg with a fork.

I start my day in simple failure.

Morning on This Street

It's Saturday with the gray
Noise of rain at the window,
Its fingers weeping to get in.
We're in bunk beds, one brother
Talking football, another
Turning to the dream girl
He'd jump from a tree to die for.
Later, in the kitchen,
He tells me, Love is like snow
Or something. I listen
With a bowl at the stove, dress,
And go outside to trees dripping
Rain, a pickup idling
With its headlights on.
I look for something to do
Slowly with a stick
In the absence of love,
That Catholic skirt in a pew.
I walk banging fences
Until Earl the Cartman rattles

Onto our block—a rope over

His shoulder. He pulls hard

Because his wife, centered

On that cart, is cold

Under the rough temple

Of cardboard he's cut for her.

Her legs are bundled in strips

Of white cloth. She's half there

With the dead, half with us

Who have oranges to give,

As he steps heavily toward

The trees they'll call

Home—a small fire and the black

Haunt of smoke. It's for his wife

That he lives and pulls a rope

To its frayed end. The sky

Is nothing and these neighbors

Wincing behind windows

Are even less. This is marriage,

A man and woman, in one kind of weather.

Evening Walk

My daughter runs outside to busy
Herself with tiny cakes of mud.
"It's important," she says,
Not wanting to hear my poor stories again.
Still I drag her to the car
And the short climb to the Berkeley
Hills, for the gardens are in bloom,
Red thing and yellow this and that.
Trees with rootfuls of clouds
Line the walk. "They're older than me,"
I say, and she won't look at them,
Or the tidy grandma houses
Quaint as teacups.

The rich seem never to come out
Of their houses. They never sit on
Lawns, or bang a ball against
The garage door, or water the green strip
Along the street—hose in one hand,
Ice tea in the other.
At our place, the petunias collapse

46

When we turn a hose on them.
Even the pepper tree, rigged
With wire and rope, fell over
Like the neck of a sick giraffe.

I talk and talk. I say the poor
Rave over the color orange
And rich yammer over egg-white.
I put this notion to Mariko, steps ahead,
A plucked branch dragging in her hand,
And begin again, me a bore to the end.
When I was like you, I picked
Grapes like nobody's business . . .
She starts to skip. I walk faster,
A loud fool. When I was a kid,
I lugged oranges and shared plums with Okies . . .
But she's on the run, a branch
Fluttering like a green fire,
Because the corner is up ahead
And an evening without me
Can't be far beyond.

How I Learned to Fly

I was tired of living on land
And envied birds in trees.
To fly among them,
I tried three kinds
Of cereal, each with
Its rocket of sugar.
I hoped I might fly
That day, something
I had wanted to do
Since I first jumped
From the doghouse.
"I know I can do it,"
I told myself at breakfast.
With a soupspoon,
I rowed cereal into my mouth,
Which was round
As a halo. I rained
A second helping into
My bowl, ate that pile,
Then sighed. I patted
My stomach, got up,
And plopped myself

It would be a trippy
experience if we humans could
fly, even if it were only in spurts.
It would have helped me escape
trouble when I was a boy.

Into a fat, fat recliner.
"I wanna fly," I whined,
"Even if it's only over
The doghouse." I turned
On, turned off, the TV.
I patted my stomach,
Which sloshed with
Milk and soggy cereal.
Then I felt a power surge
In my legs, my arms,
And rolled my hands
Into fists as my hair
Stood up. A sugar rush!
I charged out of the house,
The sugar tripping through
My chicken-thin legs.
I swear my feet lifted
Off the sidewalk, not once,
Not twice, but every time
I lifted my featherless arms.
Even the robins, normally oblivious,
Dropped their worms
To look at me in brotherly awe.
I was flying.

Some Words
about Time

Bored, I open the back of an ancient clock

And the minutes pile out,

Exhausted from spinning

Out the same hammered seconds.

The minutes stagger on the table

And collapse, for they are dizzy,

For they have realized they have no legs,

For the surface of the table is flat

And what have they known but a round world.

I touch one of the minutes—an ant

With feeling antennae—and with my hand

Bulldoze them all to the kitchen floor.

Again, I am bored. I examine the oily guts

Of the clock, tinker with the sprockets

And springs, and revel in the master plan

To keep lackeys punching the clock.

I think of myself at the car wash

Bringing a soapy sponge to

The toothy grille of an old Pontiac.

I used four seconds on each of the dirty teeth,
And ten seconds on each droopy headlight.
This was how I viewed time
At age seventeen, the boy in morning
Sunlight and, two minutes to eight,
Reaching for a sponge,
Sponge that was a wheezing lung—
Even before the clock started
My hand struggled with an exhausted tool.

Door-to-Door

My mother was selling Avon,

And the neighbor with a thorny bush in front,

Said, Wipe your feet and I'll listen. So

We entered her house of twice-steeped tea bags

And a cold floor furnace. The sofa

Was wrapped in clear plastic,

And the lampshades sported cellophane.

The canary in the cage was feathers on cardboard,

A better buy than a real one. The woman

Was the one who sang, Cheap! Cheap!

Mom said something about smelling good,

And the woman peeled back a pleat on her neck

And said, This is where I put lemon.

Lemon don't cost me. I got a tree

In the yard, and a tree only takes water.

The woman had the face you get

When you suck a lemon. Then the woman

Showed us a fancy box of Valentine sweets,

The biggest I had ever seen,

But she didn't offer us a single candy.
When I want good smells,
I sniff this, she said, and added,
It was a gift from a boyfriend.
I swallowed. I wanted to say,
You're too old for a boyfriend,
But she continued and said,
That was ten years ago. The candies
Are no good but I still have the smell.
I don't need no Avon.

Out the door, I asked Mom,
What kind of candy was the round one?
Chewy, she answered, and I chewed
On that answer as we worked the block.
No matter how much I swallowed,
I couldn't get the bitter taste of
That woman out of my mouth.

Envying the Children of San Francisco

At a city square

Children laugh in the red

Sweaters of Catholics,

As they walk home between trucks

And sunlight angling off buildings that end in points.

I'm holding an apple, among shoppers

Clutching bags big enough to crawl in,

And the air is warm for October—

Torn pieces of paper

Scuttle like roaches a burst at a time.

The children are careful at the lights—

The sister takes her brother's hand.

They cross looking

At their watches, and I cross, too.

I want to know where

They're going, what door they'll push open

And call home—the TV coming on,
Milk, and a cookie for each hand.

As a kid I wanted to live
In the city, in a building that rose above it all,
The gray streets burst open, a rattle
Of jackhammers. I wanted to stare down
From the eighteenth floor, and let things go—
My homework for one, a paper plane
With a half-drawn heart and a girl's name.
I wanted to say that I ate
And slept, ate and slept in a building
That faced other buildings, a sliver of sea
Blue in the distance.

I wanted to hear voices
Behind walls, the *click-click* of a poodle
Strolling to his bowl—a violin like fingers
Running down a blackboard.
I wanted to warm my hands at a teakettle
And comb my hair in an elevator, my mouth
Still stuffed with cereal, as I started off
For school, a row of pens in my shirt pocket.
Back home at the window
I wanted it to be December—

Flags and honking cars,
A Santa Claus with his pot, a single red
Balloon let go and racing skyward,
And the tiny mothers who would come around
Buildings, disappear, and come around again,
Hugging bags for all they were worth to children.

Manuel and the Football Scrubs

Three guys hung on to Manuel's right leg
As if begging him to stay.
Yet he walked across the goal line,
The football like a meatball tucked under his arm.

Manuel was huge, his shadow cold
When you stood in its freezing climate. You would think,
He can't be smart. But he would sit in
A tiny desk in front of Mr. Basmajian's large desk,
A grade-A student.

We let go of Manuel
And composed new teams,
Just me, Jaime, and Manuel against the other five.

"Go out, Soto," Manuel said.
My chance to be a hero, I thought,
And ran to the edge of the lawn,
My hurtling footsteps still in the darkness of his shadow.

—————

Arm cocked, he yelled, "Go, farther!"
I ran until I stopped at the end of the block.
He was a large speck among smaller specks.

"No, *really* farther," he bellowed.
I ran like a squirrel across the busy street
And found myself sitting on a park bench
Next to an old man with puny kneecaps.
Had he been sitting there thirty years? Forty?

Poor old guy. His hands jerked on his lap.
Was he benched like me but still wondering,
The football—when will they pass it to me?

Teaching Numbers

The moon is one,
The early stars a few more . . .
The sycamore is lean
With sparrows, four perhaps,
Three hunched like hoods
And one by itself, wiping a beak
In the rag of his shoulder.

From where we sit
We could count to a thousand
By pointing at oranges
On trees, bright lanterns
Against the dusk, globes
Of water that won't come down.

Follow me with this, then:
A stray on two legs
At a trash can, one kite in a tree,
And a couple with four hands,
Three in pockets and one scratching
An ear busy with sound:
Door, cat, scrambling leaf.

I've never been good at math. I know nothing about algebra, and calculus would hurt my brain. But I knew enough to begin to teach my daughter to count to one hundred.

(The world understands numbers,
And at birth we're not given much.
When we're lowered into the earth
We're even less, a broken
Toy of 108 bones and 23 teeth
That won't stop laughing.)

But let's not talk about this.
For the dog is happy with an eggshell
And oranges are doing wonders
At this hour in the trees.
There is popcorn to pick
From my small bowl of hands.

Let's start again
With numbers that will help.

The moon is one,
The early stars a few more . . .

How Things Work

Our young daughter was always asking impossibly difficult questions. Where do the stars come from? Why is the world round? How come we sleep at night? I could answer some of the questions, and others I couldn't—like the questions about the economy of our nation.

Today it's going to cost us thirty-five dollars
To live. Six for a softball. Eight for a book,
A handful of ones for coffee and two sweet rolls,
Bus fare, rosin for your mother's violin.
We're completing our task. The tip I left
For the waitress filters down
Like rain, wetting the new roots of a child
Perhaps, a belligerent cat that won't let go
Of a balled sock until there's chicken to eat.
As far as I can tell, daughter, it works like this:
You buy crayons from a stationer, a bag of apples
From the farmers market, and what dollars
Are passed on help others buy pencils, a guitar,
Tickets to a matinee movie.
If we buy a goldfish, someone tries on a hat.
If we buy crayons, someone walks home with a broom.
A tip, a small purchase here and there,
And things just keep going. I guess.

Pepper Tree

We tapped you into a snug hole,
Staked you to a piece
Of lumber that was once part of our house,
A rail from the back porch;
That, too, was a tree, cut,
Milled, and slapped with wire
For shipment, back in the 1930s.
Don't worry. You're not going anywhere.
The wind comes, the sparrows come—
The rain falls pointlessly against branches,
Notched with a promise of leaves.
You are here, under rain
And the rain of *Get big, little tree*,
From our daughter.

The truth is I don't care
For the street where we live, the banged-up
Cars and motor oil poured into drains,
Loud people with loud radios, the scuttle of bags
Blowing from the grocery called Lucky Day.
I don't care for the billboard,

And the messy telephone wires.

I want to look at you, pepper tree,

Green and moving like the sea

In wind. I want you to grow

Heavy with sparrows and spring's first robins.

Or perhaps a gull will circle over

Our house, settle in your branches,

And scream for the sea. So I stake

You to the front yard and splash you with water.

You're thin as my daughter's wrist,

Your branches are like her arms.

Stand up, little tree, bend with the wind,

Be here tomorrow.

The Boy's First Flight

One side of our house was desert
And the other, the one facing east, was Eden itself.
I didn't know this until I bounced on a trampoline
And landed on the garage roof, me the unpaid astronaut,
Age nine, knees scuffed from a rough landing.
I looked about, stunned. A breeze lived
In the sycamore and a single-engine airplane
Hung by a thread of exhaust in the darkening sky.
This was 1961. I asked, "Is this for us?" meaning the bushel
Of stars, pitched and pulsating their icy thorns.
The moon was a tiger's tooth,
Hooked in a frightening way. I walked back
And forth on the roof, arms out for balance.
I saw my cat and dog, and they saw me, perhaps in awe,
Because they did lift their eyes.

And now it's 1999, the end of the millennium,
And it's certainly the end of my knees,
Whose springs are long gone. A latch of rust groans
In each knee—
How they would love that payload of a taut trampoline.

I see these children, how they jump, fall back, and jump again.
If only I could sit on a roof, in summer,
If only I could watch a Shuttle—what lever
Does the commander push
To make a smile on his face, her face? I'm in the dark, literally,
Ice cubes rattling in my tea. The crickets sing in the weeds,
And soon the Shuttle, dime-bright, will lift off
And pull away. My friends, my suited-up pilgrims,
What news will you bring?

Jackie was a childhood friend.
One summer evening we sat on the
grass talking about whom we would
end up marrying. Each of us had a
clear notion of the ideal girl, and
each of us thought the
other was wrong.

Brown Girl,
Blonde Okie

Jackie and I sit cross-legged

In the yard, plucking at

Grass, cupping flies

And shattering them against

Each other's faces,

And then smiling that it's summer,

No school, and we can

Sleep out under stars

And the blink of jets

Crossing up our lives.

The flies leave, or die,

And we're in the dark,

Still cross-legged.

We talk not dogs or baseball,

But who we will love,

What brown girl or blonde

Okie to open up to

And say we are sorry

For our faces, the filth

We shake from our hair,

The teeth without direction.

"We're *really* ugly," says Jackie

On one elbow, and stares

Lost between jets

At what this might mean.

In the dark I touch my

Nose, trace my lips,

And pinch my mouth

Into a dull flower.

Dang, we're in trouble.

Chatting with Gary Soto

Question: *Where do your poems come from?*

Gary Soto: They come from my memory or from a story someone told me; they come from feelings and the inventive side of the mind. Most of the poems in this collection come from real experiences. But, like other artists, I treat the experiences with a measure of creativity.

Q: *Then, not everything in your narrative poems is true?*

GS: No. But most poets who tell stories through verse believe that poems should be credible, that the experiences in them should be possible in life even if they did not happen to the poet. For instance, in "Learning to Bargain" my friend didn't really kill the cat. As I remember, he heaved a brick at it because it had knocked over his garbage can. Luckily, he missed. Still, I didn't like the idea of trying to hurt the cat. I threatened to tell his mom if he ever did it again. In the poem, I make our actions more ominous. I say that he killed the cat and that I threatened to tell unless he paid me a dime. I wanted to show in the poem that people start conspiring at a very early age.

Q: *Do all poems tell stories?*

GS: No. A lyric poem expresses the feelings or thoughts of the poem's speaker. (The speaker does not have to be the poet.) A lyric poem does not tell a complete story, as a narrative poem does. It offers impressions. "October" is a lyric poem.

Q: *Does a poet ever imitate other poets?*

GS: No poet works alone. Poets often have literary influences—my own work can be traced to the work of Pablo Neruda, for instance—and occasionally poets will pay homage to poets by writing in their style. Christopher Smart, the eighteenth-century English poet, wrote a longish poem titled "Jubilate Agno" (Latin for "Rejoice in the Lamb"). He composed this poem while in an asylum; one section of this poem dwells on his cat, Jeoffry, whom Smart loved dearly for its pranks and natural abilities. So I, too, have written my cat poem in the shape and playfulness of Smart's poem.

Q: *Do you have to get inspired to write?*

GS: When I first began writing in the early 1970s, I waited to be "inspired," which for me was a physical sensation—my body tingled. Now I get this feeling less frequently. I doodle a few phrases or lines, and a nice feeling settles on my shoulders. This is a sign that I'm ready to write. It's the same with an artist friend of mine. Sometimes she doesn't know what she's going to paint until she sketches a few lines, maybe a face, maybe an outline of a tree. Then, suddenly, like the flash of a camera, she has a subject and a feeling settles on her shoulders, too.

Q: *When do you write?*

GS: Each poet has a routine. I write in the morning when my mind is clear and I can concentrate. These days I use a laptop computer, but I recall when I wrote using a pencil and a notepad. Also, I discovered that I do most of my writing during December and January when winter has forced me inside and I have to do something with these hours of mine.

Q: *Do you ever change any of your words?*

GS: Because most poems are short, compared to other kinds of literature such as the novel, every line needs a great deal of concentration. I once worked on a single fourteen-line poem for a week, changing verbs, reworking line breaks, cutting out unnecessary words.

Q: *Do you have a favorite poem?*

GS: Yes, but I don't tell the other poems because I don't want to show favoritism. My favorite poem is "Hitchhiking with a Friend." The poem is about wonderment and the personal history goes like this: I was nineteen, bored, and looking to get out of Fresno during spring break. I had never hitchhiked in my life until a friend, also named Gary, suggested that we thumb a ride to Pismo Beach, ninety-five miles from Fresno. We stood at the edge of the road outside Fresno, near an area called Malaga, and waited and waited. Two hours later a truck driver picked us up, took us a short distance, and dropped us off near a dairy. After a short wait there, a man in a banged-up truck picked us up and soon we were riding over the coastal mountains with the wind in our faces.

Q: *Do you write the titles of your poems first?*

GS: I usually come up with a title when I'm about halfway finished with a poem. A title often hints to the reader what the poem is about. At times, however, poets will use a wild title that they may not wholly understand but may like for the way it sounds or the way it looks on the page. An example is "How You Gave Up Root Beer." It's a strange title that doesn't seem "poetic" yet has some intrigue.

Q: *Why are poems sometimes difficult to understand?*

GS: Poetry is a concentrated form of writing; so much meaning is packed into such a little space. Therefore, each word in a poem is important and is chosen very carefully to convey just the right meaning. For example, the word *tree* might stand for more than a tree in an orchard. It might symbolize life itself, or it might symbolize the strength of your grandfather or your father. *Rain* may symbolize tears; *dusk* may symbolize approaching death.

Another reason why poetry can be difficult to understand is that you're not used to reading it. The more you read it, the better you get at understanding words and lines.

Q: *Should I read a poem more than once?*

GS: Go for it! Read it again and again. One poet remarked that "poetry is an act of attention." In other words, you have to concentrate when you read a poem, just as you might concentrate when you're in the batter's box and your team needs you to bring in a player on second base.

I also like to think of a poem as meeting a new person. Just because you say hello once doesn't mean that you never want to see this person again. Of course you do. A poem also needs to be seen again and again.

Q: *Why don't your poems rhyme?*

GS: Most poets today don't use rhyme and meter; they write "free verse"—poetry that has no regular rhyme or rhythm. Poetry has changed over the years, but a poet's motives for writing haven't changed. Most of us write because we feel something and want to share it with others.

Q: *When did you decide to become a poet?*

GS: In the introduction I mention encountering Gregory Corso's poem "Marriage" in a contemporary American poetry anthology, and the wildness of his imagery both baffled and exhilarated me. However, I was truly smitten after I read a bittersweet poem by Edward Field called "Unwanted." It's about a lonely man who feels sad that no one wants him. He hangs a picture of himself at the post office next to posters of dangerous criminals. He wants people to recognize him and love him. I was inspired by this poem and identified with it because it seemed to speak about my own life at the time. I read the poem over and over, and even typed it out to see what it looked like. I read this poet's book and began to read other poets. After a while, I decided to write my own poems, and I have been doing it ever since.